ABUNDANT TRUTH INTERNATIONAL MINISTRIES

_____

Restoration and Recovery Series

_____

The God of Another Chance

Overcoming Your Failures: Possessing Your Divine Destiny

Roderick Levi Evans

The God of Another Chance

Overcoming Your Failures: Possessing Your Divine Destiny
All Rights Reserved © 2014 by Roderick L. Evans

No part of this book may be reproduced or transmitted in any form or by any means, graphic, electronic, or mechanical, including photocopying, recording, taping, or by any information storage or retrieval system, without the permission in writing from the publisher.

Front & Back Cover Designs by Abundant Truth Publishing

Abundant Truth Publishing
an imprint of Abundant Truth International Ministries

For information address:
Abundant Truth International
P.O. Box 126
Camden, NC 27921

Unless otherwise indicated all of the scripture quotations are taken from the Authorized King James Version of the Bible. Scripture quotations marked with NIV are taken from the New International Version of the Bible. Scriptures marked with NASV are taken for the New American Standard Version of the Bible.

978-1601413017

Printed in the United States of America

Contents

Introduction

Chapter 1 – What is this that thou hast done? 1

    Adam's Transgression 4

    Adam's Troubles 13

    Adam's Triumph 22

Chapter 2 – Where is Abel thy brother? 33

    Cain's Compromise and Complaint 37

    Cain's Counsel and Conspiracy 44

Contents (cont.)

Cain's Carnage and Curse   48

Cain's Comfort and City   58

Chapter 3 – Why came we forth out of Egypt?   69

   Israel's Exile   72

   Israel's Exodus   78

   Israel's Example   86

   Israel's Entrance   93

Chapter 4 – Wilt thou be made whole?   99

   Forget the Pain   104

Contents (cont.)

Focus on Christ   108

Follow after Righteousness   112

Bibliography   119

Introduction

The books of Psalms and Proverbs present two phenomenal statements regarding the believer's life. The first is found in Psalms 34:19, "Many are the afflictions of the righteous: but the LORD delivereth him out of them all."

The second is found in Proverbs 24:16, "For a just man falleth seven times, and riseth up again: but the wicked shall fall into mischief."

Each of these statements reveal the

troubles that believers will face and how it is possible for unforeseen mistakes and failures to come. However, the strength of the second admonition is that the righteous will get up after times of failure and defeat.

The Restoration and Recovery Series was developed to bring hope, comfort, and peace to Christians during and after troublesome times in their Christan walk.

In this Publication

How do you handle your failures? Do you allow them to paralyze your personal growth and happiness? Or, do you learn from them? The Bible contains numerous accounts of individuals who failed in their relationship with Him. Yet, this did not prevent them from doing great things for Him.

God is the God of another chance. He will ensure that the good work that He has started in you will be completed. In the second book of the Restoration and Recovery Series, we will examine the failures and ultimate successes of biblical characters.

If they overcame, then, the Christian today can come out of any personal Egypt and enter into their promised Canaan. Their examples provide hope and strength for the Christian today. Book 2 of 4.

-Chapter 1-

What Is This That Thou Hast Done?

THE GOD OF ANOTHER CHANCE

God asked this question to Eve after the transgression. Sin entered the world by one man, Adam. Adam's formation was the crown of God's creation. He created man in His likeness and image.

So God created man in his own image, in the image of God created he him; male and female created he them. (Genesis 1:27)

Adam was to represent and reflect God's authority and character, respectively. As long as Adam followed one command, He would not fail in His service.

> And the Lord God commanded the man, saying, Of every tree of the garden thou mayest freely eat: But of the tree of the knowledge of good and evil, thou shalt not eat of it: for in the day that thou eatest thereof thou shalt surely die. (Genesis 2:16-17)

However, Adam disobeyed God's commandment.

Adam's Transgression

There are theologians who blame

Adam's transgression upon Eve. Some suppose that Eve seduced Adam into eating the fruit. This is contrary to the biblical account and subsequent history. In the book of Genesis, we discover that no record of seduction took place; Eve simply gave it to Adam.

And when the woman saw that the tree was good for food, and that it was pleasant to the eyes, and a tree to be desired to make one wise, she took of the fruit thereof, and did eat, and gave also unto her husband with her; and he did eat. (Genesis 3:6)

The Bible records that Eve *GAVE* it to Adam and he ate. When God confronted Adam, he said that the fruit was given to him.

And the man said, The woman whom thou gavest to be with me, she gave me of the tree, and I did eat. (Genesis 3:12)

Adam's transgression was greater than Eve's for two reasons. The first is that God spoke the commandment to

Adam personally. He knew firsthand what the Lord commanded. The second reason is that Eve transgressed the commandment through the serpent's deception. However, Adam wasn't deceived, he was outright disobedient.

> *But, I fear, lest by any means, as the serpent beguiled (tricked) Eve through his subtlety... (II Corinthians 11:3, Parenthesis mine)*
>
> *And Adam was not deceived, but the woman being deceived was in the transgression. (I Timothy 2:14)*

THE GOD OF ANOTHER CHANCE

Adam willingly disobeyed God's command. There are times when the believer willingly disobeys God's command. Afterwards, God confronted him.

And he said, Who told thee that thou wast naked? Hast thou eaten of the tree, whereof I commanded thee that thou shouldest not eat? And the man said, The woman whom thou gavest to be with me, she gave me of the tree, and I did eat. (Genesis 3:11-12)

However, the believer is not to respond like Adam with blame shifting and excuses. *In order to overcome our transgressions, we have to confess them.* David states,

> *Behold, thou desirest truth in the inward parts: and in the hidden part thou shalt make me to know wisdom. (Psalm 51:6)*

The believer has to be honest about areas of weakness and temptation. If not, there will be no subsequent victory in these areas. Adam's transgression was done willingly. It was the direct result of the devil's initial seduction of Eve. This demonstrates that two areas of warfare are consistently upon the believer. The first is the believer's flesh.

Eve submitted to the serpent's deception because the fruit was good for food, pleasant to the eyes, and gave 'wisdom.' These three things appeal to man's flesh.

And when the woman saw that the tree was good for food, and that it was pleasant to the eyes, and a tree to be desired to make one wise, she took of the fruit thereof, and did eat, and gave also unto her husband with her; and he did eat. (Genesis 3:6)

The fruit could satisfy hunger (it probably tasted good). The fruit inspired desire in those that looked upon it. It also offered intellectual stimulation.

These attributes of the fruit had to contribute to Adam's deliberate violation of God's command since no enticement from Eve is recorded.

The second area of warfare from Eve's deception and Adam's transgression was demonic influence. Adam's transgression was the direct result of the serpent's deception. *Every believer has to realize that the enemy will use the flesh, in most cases, to cause sin and failure in his/her relationship with the Lord.*

Just as the serpent was seductive in his presentation to Eve, he will be subtle in his attack against the believer. If the believer is not watchful, he will enter into temptation and a snare of the devil.

Adam's Troubles

The Bible is clear that Adam transgressed God's command with dire consequences. The first is that Adam found himself naked before the Lord. Sin will cause the believer to feel naked before God and man.

Aside from feelings of guilt and shame (nakedness), the believer experiences the same penalties as Adam in a measure. God's discipline upon Adam was four-fold.

And unto Adam he said, Because

THE GOD OF ANOTHER CHANCE

thou hast hearkened unto the voice of thy wife, and hast eaten of the tree, of which I commanded thee, saying, Thou shalt not eat of it: cursed is the ground for thy sake; in sorrow shalt thou eat of it all the days of thy life; Thorns also and thistles shall it bring forth to thee; and thou shalt eat the herb of the field; In the sweat of thy face shalt thou eat bread, till thou return unto the ground; for out of it wast thou taken: for dust thou art, and unto dust shalt thou return. (Genesis 3:17-19)

He was expelled from the Garden. Adam and Eve lost their home in Eden. Because of disobedience, they would no longer experience the peace of the garden. When a believer sins, he experiences separation from God in a measure. Though God will not reject or disown the believer, fellowship is partially broken.

But your iniquities have separated between you and your God, and

THE GOD OF ANOTHER CHANCE

your sins have hid his face from you, that he will not hear. (Isaiah 59:2)

Like Adam, sins and failures cause us to be ejected from the presence of God. It becomes difficult to discern His presence and receive His peace. However, this can be reversed with confession and repentance.

The ground was cursed. In the Garden, Adam tilled the ground and it brought forth fruit. Now, when Adam tilled the ground, it would produce things that he was not accustomed to. His toils and labors would become arduous and burdensome. The same applies to believers. The scriptures declare that the way of a transgressor is hard.

> *Good understanding giveth favour: but the way of transgressors is hard. (Proverbs 13:5)*

When a believer sins, the ordinances of God are transgressed. Thus, the believer becomes a transgressor. Instead of walking in God's favor, the ground (life) seems to be cursed. The believer's way seems to become more difficult.

Adam would eat the fruit of the ground in sorrow. Not only was the ground cursed, but Adam would eat from it in sorrow. In addition, the ground would produce thorns and thistles. Sin causes the believer to live in sorrow and regret.

The thorns and thistles produced by the ground represent the constant feelings of guilt and shame experienced when one fails. Adam's curse lasted as long as he lived.

The believer will experience these

things as long as no confession and repentance takes place.

When I kept silence, my bones waxed old through my roaring all the day long. For day and night thy hand was heavy upon me: my moisture is turned into the drought of summer. Selah. (Psalm 2:3-4)

David stated that when he did not confess his sin, he suffered. There was no joy in his life (moisture turned into drought) and conviction was upon him (Thy hand was heavy upon me). He lived in sorrow until his confession.

The believer will experience thorns and thistles coupled with feelings of sorrow and regret until sin and failure is confessed.

Adam would eat bread with sweat in his face. The ground was cursed, producing thorns and thistles. In addition, when Adam ate bread, sweat would be in his face. Believers experience the same while known sins are not confessed. In the scriptures, Jesus made the word of God comparable to bread.

But he answered and said, It is written, Man shall not live by bread alone, but by every word that proceedeth out of the mouth of God. (Matthew 4:4)

This implies that when a believer hears the word of God (eat bread) and there is a known sin, they will stand in fear of God's judgment (in the sweat of thy face).

Though Adam experienced troubles because of his transgression, there was also triumph. Adam's disobedience did not lead to his ultimate demise and shame but ended in glory and honor.

Adam's Triumph

Adam's transgression subjected humanity to sin. His transgression had some dire consequences.

> *Wherefore, as by one man sin entered into the world, and death by sin; and so death passed upon 3all men, for that all have sinned. (Romans 5:12)*

Believers may experience the consequences of sin, but this does not *mean that God's plan for their lives will not happen.* Adam's transgression ultimately ended in triumph. Adam's triumph demonstrates how the believer will overcome sin and failure.

After pronouncing judgment upon the woman, God said that the seed of the woman would crush the head of the serpent. However, we understand that the woman can have no seed without the man.

Thus, Adam's seed would triumph over the serpent. Though Adam's sin produced sin in his descendants (seed), his seed would eventually overcome. This reveals that the believer can still triumph over all the works and temptations of the devil.

> *Behold, I give unto you power to tread on serpents and scorpions, and over all the power of the enemy: and nothing shall by any means hurt you. (Luke 10:19)*

Though the enemy may manipulate believers into sin through subtlety, they can overcome him. If Adam's seed would eventually be victorious, the believer will overcome if he continues to follow the Lord. Proverbs declares,

> *For a just man falleth seven times, and riseth up again. (Proverbs 24:16)*

A sign of righteousness in the believer is that after he falls (sins), he gets up again. Adam's triumph reached its full manifestation in Christ. Christ not only reversed the work of the first Adam, but He also redeemed Adam's name.

> *For as by one man's disobedience many were made sinners, so by the*

obedience of one shall many be made righteous. (Romans 5:19)

Through His ministry, Christ overturned the first Adam's transgression. Adam made men sinners, but Christ made men righteous. This shows that God can reverse the effects of the believer's sins and failures. He did not allow humanity to live forever in the bondage of sin caused by Adam.

This encourages believers to know that God will not always allow the consequences of sin to rule in their lives.

He is merciful. He delights in mercy.

> *For as in Adam all die, even so in Christ shall all be made alive. (I Corinthians 15:22)*

Adam was a type of Christ. Though he failed, Christ would succeed. In his writings, Paul called Christ the last Adam.

> *And so it is written, The first man Adam was made a living soul; the last Adam was made a quickening spirit. (I Corinthians 15:45)*

Thus, Christ brought honor to Adam's name. He reversed the effects of his sin and removed the stigma attached to his name by taking on his name. God does the same for the believer. If the believer continues to walk with God after he sins, he will restore honor to the believer's name.

Adam's transgression ended in triumph and so will the believer's if he/she continues in Him. Though believers may experience the effects and consequences of sin, it does not negate God's plan and purpose for their lives. God is gracious.

For he saith to Moses, I will have mercy on whom I will have mercy, and I will have compassion on whom I will have compassion. So then it is not of him that willeth, nor of him that runneth, but of God that sheweth mercy. (Romans 9:15-16)

THE GOD OF ANOTHER CHANCE

Notes:

_____

_____

_____

_____

_____

_____

_____

_____

_____

_____

THE GOD OF ANOTHER CHANCE

-Chapter 2-

Where Is Abel Thy Brother?

THE GOD OF ANOTHER CHANCE

The story of Cain and Abel is both common and controversial. It is an account of 'firsts.' This story introduces us to the first form of sacrifice and worship of God. It is the first account of sibling rivalry.

Most importantly, it is the first account of murder in human history. Although this story is sad, there are lessons to be learned. In addition, we discover that this story does not end in tragedy for Cain.

We discover that God's legacy of patience, longsuffering, and love are revealed in His interaction with Cain.

As we examine Cain's character, great truth for believers today will be exposed. After man's expulsion from the Garden, Eve conceived and brought forth two sons. The first was named Cain and the second was named Abel. There is no biblical record of their formative years. Yet, the Bible draws our attention to each man's occupation and worship.

And Abel was a keeper of sheep, but Cain was a tiller of the ground. (Genesis 4:2b)

Abel was a keeper of sheep (shepherd), while Cain was a tiller of the ground (farmer). Each man brought an offering unto the Lord based upon his occupation.

Cain's Compromise & Complaint

From the biblical account, it is discovered that Abel's offering was preferred above Cain's.

And in process of time it came to pass, that Cain brought of the fruit of the ground an offering unto the Lord. And Abel, he also brought of the firstlings of his flock and of the fat thereof. And the Lord had respect unto Abel and to his offering: But unto Cain and to his offering he had not respect. And Cain was very wroth, and his countenance fell. (Genesis 4:3-5)

The Bible is not clear as to why; however, we can successfully establish the reasons. When speaking of Abel's sacrifice, the Bible declares that he brought the firstlings of his flock. This means that he offered the best of his flock.

> *By faith Abel offered unto God a more excellent sacrifice than Cain, by which he obtained witness that he was righteous, God testifying of his gifts: and by it he being dead yet speaketh. (Hebrews 11:4)*

Cain's offering does not have the same implications surrounding it. The account only reveals that he brought of the fruit of the ground. It does not say he brought the first fruits or the best. Thus, Cain compromised in his relationship with the Lord. He did not offer God his best, but he wanted the best from God.

Some believers today, like Cain, are living in compromise. They offer to God the 'leftovers' in their lives. God is not first. They only pray in times of need. They read their Bibles when it is convenient. They only stand for what is right when it is beneficial to them.

Examine yourselves, whether ye be in the faith; prove your own selves. (II Corinthians 13:5a)

Some reading this book can identify

with the above. *Compromise goes beyond the standards that an individual has.* One can have standards, but no demonstration. *To avoid compromise, knowledge has to be accompanied with qualifying activities.*

Cain knew that he was to bring God an offering, but his works did not reflect his knowledge. The consequence was that God preferred his brother's offering above his own. This produced internal turmoil and complaint within Cain.

The Bible says that Cain became angry and his countenance fell. He became sad. On the inside, he became envious of his brother. Rather than change the manner of his offering, he focused on his brother. He blamed his brother for God's rejection of his offering. He felt that if his brother were out of the way, God would accept his offering.

Not as Cain, who was of that wicked one, and slew his brother. And wherefore slew he him? Because his own works were evil, and his brother's righteous. (I John 3:12)

This scenario is repeated in churches today. *Some believers are envious of God's interaction and dealings with their brothers and sisters.* When one is in compromise, he will view others as enemies. *Whatever good they see someone else perform; they believe it is done to make them look bad (or unspiritual).* This is partially true. When one is in compromise, another individual's good works will expose their unrighteousness. Cain and Abel's story exemplifies this.

Cain's Counsel & Conspiracy

Because of his inner turmoil, God spoke to him. Though Cain's offering was unacceptable, the Lord's words to him were full of compassion and concern. He did not want Cain's inner conflict to produce sin. God knew the murderous intent that was developing in Cain's subconscious.

And the Lord said unto Cain, Why art thou wroth? and why is thy countenance fallen? If thou doest well, shalt thou not be accepted? and if thou doest not well, sin lieth at the door. And unto thee shall be his desire, and thou shalt rule over him. (Genesis 4:6-7)

God's counsel to Cain was simple. Cain only had to do well (bring the right offering) and he would be accepted. If he did not do this, sin would rule over him. The same applies to the believer.

The Holy Spirit convicts the believer of sin, righteousness, and judgment. *If the believer repents and does well (walk in righteousness), God will accept him and bless him.* However, if the believer does not confess his sin, sin will rule over him. This is an affront to the work of Jesus Christ. He came that sin would no longer reign in the believer's life.

> *Let not sin therefore reign in your mortal body, that ye should obey it in the lusts thereof. (Romans 6:12)*

Cain did not respond properly to God's counsel. Believers have to guard against rejecting the counsel of

THE GOD OF ANOTHER CHANCE

God. *When the believer is wrong, he must be willing to acknowledge and forsake any known wickedness and evil intent.*

Sin must not blind the believer like it did Cain. Even after the Lord's warning, Cain allowed his envy to fuel his conspiracy to murder his brother.

Before continuing our examination, one point has to be made. *To walk in envy is sin.* Envy will lead to sin. These two things have damaged the lives of many believers. Some believers experience these emotions often. Rather than confess and forsake them, they cover them up. When this occurs, criticism and confusion surface among believers.

For where envying and strife is, there is confusion and every evil work. (James 3:16)

If you find it hard to compliment others and appreciate their labors in the Lord, you may be struggling with envy. Do not allow it to dominate you as it did Cain.

Cain's Carnage & Curse

Cain rejected God's counsel and acted upon his internal conspiracy to kill his brother.

> *And Cain talked with Abel his brother: and it came to pass, when they were in the field, that Cain rose up against Abel his brother, and slew him. (Genesis 4:8)*

The Bible does not tell us how Cain did it. It gives no description of technique or tool used. After these events, God comes to Cain and asks, "Where is Abel thy brother?"

> *And the Lord said unto Cain, Where is Abel thy brother? And he said, I*

know not: am I my brother's keeper? (Genesis 4:9)

Cain responded with a lie and another question. First, he says that he does not know where Abel is. Then, he continues by asking the famous question, "Am I my brother's keeper?"

In this section, the word *carnage* is used to describe Cain's murder of Abel. It is because Cain shed Abel's blood. After the Lord confronts him, He states that Abel's blood cries to Him from the ground.

And he said, What hast thou done? the voice of thy brother's blood crieth unto me from the ground. (Genesis 4:10)

Since Cain did not confess his error, the Lord reveals that He knows what was done. Following this, God pronounces His judgment and curse upon Cain.

And now art thou cursed from the earth, which hath opened her mouth to receive thy brother's blood from thy hand; When thou tillest the ground, it shall not henceforth yield unto thee her strength; a fugitive and a vagabond shalt thou be in the earth. (Genesis 4:11-12)

Since Cain polluted the earth with his brother's blood, he was now cursed from the earth. If he tried to continue to till the earth and grow crops, he would not be successful. Cain's sin affected his life and way of living. His sin caused his whole life to change.

He could no longer do what he was accustomed to doing. He no longer could be a tiller of the ground with success and

THE GOD OF ANOTHER CHANCE

Cain would be a fugitive and vagabond for the rest of his life.

When the believer sins, there may be irreversible consequences, at times. This is determined by the ultimate will of God.

Cain could no longer till the earth. His works would be futile. *In certain cases, believers may have to experience life-altering situations because of sin.* However, God's discipline upon Cain served a greater purpose than punishment.

All of Cain's disobedience arose from his occupation. He was a tiller of the ground, but his offering was unacceptable. We established that he brought the Lord his leftovers. Thus, he valued the fruit of his labor above God.

God's discipline upon him would keep him from being subjected to the same error. *In some cases, God will allow permanent consequences for sin to remain in the life of believers to ensure they will not return to it.*

Another point of interest is that

THE GOD OF ANOTHER CHANCE

Cain's punishment did not involve his death. God said that he was cursed from the earth and that he was a fugitive and vagabond. God did not tell Cain that because he slew Abel, he was going to be killed.

Cain feared that someone would kill him because of his actions. *Some fear that because they did something to someone, it will happen to them in return.* This is not always true.

Be not deceived; God is not mocked: for whatsoever a man soweth, that shall he also reap. For he that soweth to his flesh shall of the flesh reap corruption; but he that soweth to the Spirit shall of the Spirit reap life everlasting. (Galatians 6:7-8)

Some are fearful because of these verses of scripture. When Paul says that one will reap what he sows, he qualifies his statement in the eighth verse. He was not saying that what one does will come back to them. However, he states that if one sows to his flesh, he will reap corruption and if to the Spirit, life everlasting.

Paul did not state these things to inspire the wrong perspective on life and God's discipline. He used these verses to encourage the people to do good works. Believers should know that the common application of these verses is somewhat misleading. Why? *God does not always allow what we have done to come back to us.* David said,

> *He hath not dealt with us after our sins; nor rewarded us according to our iniquities. (Psalm 103:10)*

THE GOD OF ANOTHER CHANCE

Cain experienced this verse. God did not reward him according to his iniquity. He committed murder, but God would not kill him. The believer experiences the same today.

Cain's Comfort & City

Some will say, "How was Cain comforted?" After God pronounced His sentence, Cain exclaimed,

And Cain said unto the Lord, My punishment is greater than I can bear. Behold, thou hast driven me out this day from the face of the

earth; and from thy face shall I be hid; and I shall be a fugitive and a vagabond in the earth; and it shall come to pass, that every one that findeth me shall slay me. (Genesis 4:13-14)

Cain laments over God's punishment. In essence, he was crying out to the Lord for some form of relief. The prophet echoed this sentiment.

O Lord, I have heard thy speech, and was afraid: O Lord, revive thy work in the midst of the years, in the

THE GOD OF ANOTHER CHANCE

midst of the years make known; in wrath remember mercy. (Habakkuk 3:2)

Habakkuk asked God to remember mercy in the midst of His wrath. This is what Cain desired of God. As we continue on, we discover that God offers Cain some comfort. He sets a seal upon him that no man would kill him. Even in judgment, God was merciful. *Believers have to remember that God will be merciful to them, even in cases of deliberate sin.* He did this for Cain; yet,

THE GOD OF ANOTHER CHANCE

how much more for those who have received His Son?

> *And the Lord said unto him, Therefore whosoever slayeth Cain, vengeance shall be taken on him sevenfold. And the Lord set a mark upon Cain, lest any finding him should kill him. (Genesis 4:15)*

God had mercy upon him in spite of the discipline. This should encourage believers to know that *God will be merciful if true confession and repentance take place.*

To end this section, one crucial element of Cain's story is worthy of note. Cain sinned. His penalty was that he could no longer be a successful tiller of the ground. However, the scriptures state that after he left God's presence, he went to Nod.

And Cain went out from the presence of the Lord, and dwelt in the land of Nod, on the east of Eden. (Genesis 4:16)

Though Cain could no longer be a tiller, he still was productive. While in the land of Nod, his wife conceived a bare him a son. In addition, he built a city and named it after his son.

And Cain knew his wife; and she conceived, and bare Enoch: and he builded a city, and called the name of the city, after the name of his son, Enoch. (Genesis 4:17)

This teaches two important truths. *The first is that if the committing of sin resulted in discipline, the believer can still be fruitful.* This is reflected in Cain becoming a father. He was able to bring forth life after his failure. *The believer can bring life to others even after sin, failure, and defeat.* Though sin may have consequences, the believer is still needed to function in the Body of Christ.

The second truth is that God will give new direction for your life if sin brought death in other areas. Cain was banned from tilling the ground, yet he built a city. He received honor for being the founder of a city. He was tiller of the ground, but he was able to do something he had not been known for.

THE GOD OF ANOTHER CHANCE

This demonstrates that failures may hinder certain activities, but God will cause your life to be productive in other areas. This is why believers should not give up after failure. God can restore purpose to your life, even after failure.

Cain's story teaches us to be aware of envy. It also teaches us that sin may have unchangeable consequences. *However, it reveals to us that there is life after failure.* If we continue in Him, He will be merciful to us even in the midst of our faults.

THE GOD OF ANOTHER CHANCE

Cain's story helps us to understand that not all is lost. *If God was merciful to him, He will be to us also.* In addition, God can turn our failures in certain areas into successes in others.

THE GOD OF ANOTHER CHANCE

Notes:

_____

_____

_____

_____

_____

_____

_____

_____

_____

_____

_____

THE GOD OF ANOTHER CHANCE

-Chapter 3-

Why Came We Forth Out of Egypt?

THE GOD OF ANOTHER CHANCE

The children of Israel repeatedly asked this question while in the wilderness. God promised to take them into Canaan. However, the difficulties they experienced caused them to doubt the fulfillment of the promise. Consequently, they repeatedly rebelled against Moses and sinned against God.

In spite of this, God brought Israel into the land of promise. In this section, we will explore Israel's Exodus from Egypt and their entrance into Canaan. If God brought them out of Egypt and into

Canaan, He will do the same for believers.

Israel's Exile

The book of Exodus introduces us to the children of Israel multiplying in the land of Egypt. Joseph's invitation to his father and brothers to come to Egypt resulted in the birth of a great nation.

> *And the children of Israel were fruitful, and increased abundantly, and multiplied, and waxed exceeding mighty; and the land was filled with them. (Exodus 1:7)*

However, the entrance of a new pharaoh marked the end of Israel's favor. Life in Egypt changed from liberty to captivity. In effect, the children of Israel were now in exile.

Therefore they did set over them taskmasters to afflict them with their burdens. And they built for Pharaoh treasure cities, Pithom and Raamses. And the Egyptians made the children of Israel to serve with rigour: And they made their lives bitter with hard bondage, in morter, and in brick, and in all manner of service in the field: all their service, wherein they made them serve, was with rigour. (Exodus 1:11, 13-14)

God had foreordained, though brutal, this new treatment of Israel. As He revealed to Abraham what was to come, God said,

And he said unto Abram, Know of a surety that thy seed shall be a stranger in a land that is not theirs, and shall serve them; and they shall afflict them four hundred

years. (Genesis 15:13)

The Lord had prophetically shown Abraham the affliction that would befall his descendants. This information introduces some key points for Christians today.

Until now, we have discussed how believers can recover from sin and failure to walk in God's plan for their lives. In this section, we want to shift our attention to believers overcoming disappointments and hardships.

Some believers are not gripped by sin,

but their outlook on life is bleak.

Because of past hardships and seemingly unanswered prayers, they fail to believe that God will fulfill promises made to them.

Israel's story reveals an important truth. *God will allow heavy afflictions and trials to come upon believers because He knows that there will be a time of deliverance.* Israel's exile was ordained of God.

The trials and tests that believers experience are ordained of God. As Israel

THE GOD OF ANOTHER CHANCE

was destined to be delivered, so are believers destined to overcome in this life.

Many are the afflictions of the righteous: but the Lord delivereth him out of them all. (Psalm 34:19)

Israel was in Egyptian bondage for approximately four hundred years before the Lord raised up Moses to deliver them. There are Christians who believe that their years of hardship, test, and trials will never end.

Yet, if God has given promises

through the Word and the prophetic spirit, the pain of the past will not hinder the promise of the future. Israel's captivity, though harsh, did not hinder God's deliverance of them.

Israel's Exodus

Though Israel's exile was prophesied, so was their deliverance. In the same prophetic discourse to Abraham, God revealed that his descendants would be freed with great substance. In addition, these descendants would inhabit all the land that was promised to Abraham.

And also that nation, whom they shall serve, will I judge: and afterward shall they come out with great substance. In the same day the Lord made a covenant with Abram, saying, Unto thy seed have I given this land, from the river of Egypt unto the great river, the river Euphrates. (Genesis 15:14, 18)

Again, this demonstrates to believers that trials and tests will come, but victory and deliverance will certainly follow them. God sent Israel into Egypt for three evident reasons.

Believers have to understand that God allows tests and trials in their lives for the same reasons.

I. Produce Fear

God allowed Israel to enter into Egyptian bondage to produce reverential fear of Him. God would demonstrate His power for Israel, which should have produced fear of Him in Israel.

If they witnessed His judgment upon the Egyptians, they would respect and reverence Him as God, who would do the same things to them if they rebelled.

Trials and tests come into the lives of believers to produce a reverential fear of God. But, this fear is to be coupled with humility. Trials and tests, and God's subsequent deliverance from them, bring the believers into a personal encounter with God's greatness and power.

Where there is no fear of God, there is no humility. Where there is no humility before God, there is no regard for His standards. Where there is no regard for His standards, there is no place of repentance, which leads to experiencing judgment at His return.

II. Produce Faith

God allowed Israel to enter into Egypt to produce faith in them. Through demonstrating His power in their impossible situation, Israel would be able to follow God wholeheartedly.

God allows believers to experience difficulties to produce faith and patience in them. James states this in his epistle,

My brethren, count it all joy when ye fall into divers temptations; Knowing this, that the trying of your faith worketh patience. (James 1:2-3)

When one experiences sickness and God heals him, faith is gained in that area. When one faces financial difficulties and the Lord provides, faith for finances is acquired.

Many believers do not submit to this process. *Situations that are designed to produce faith have inadvertently produced frustration and depression in some.* Believers must realize that God has everything under control and will be faithful until the end.

III. Produce Fervor

Israel's Egyptian bondage came to produce future fervor in their relationship with the Lord.

The fervor that they were to possess would stem from appreciation of the Lord's deliverance. While in the wilderness or in Canaan, they would be able to remember His mercy and power, causing them to serve Him in obedience and gladness.

And remember that thou wast a servant in the land of Egypt, and that the Lord thy God brought thee out thence through a mighty hand and by a stretched out arm. (Deuteronomy 5:15a)

Believers experience hardships, which should produce fervor and not frustration. The remembrance of the trials and God's deliverance is designed to produce zeal, not anxiety.

Israel's Exodus was designed to show that God could do anything, regardless of the situation and opposition. Their exile led to their Exodus. Upon their exit (Exodus), Israel witnesses God's power as He executed judgment upon Pharaoh and Egypt.

When believers are put in impossible situations, God is orchestrating an Exodus (deliverance) that glorifies Him and His power.

Israel's Example

Though Israel's Exile and Exodus

were accompanied by God's presence and power, Israel experienced more of God's testing and deliverance. However, the example they set was not good. Believers are expected to learn from their failures and emulate their successes as recorded in the Law.

Paul wrote,

> *Now all these things happened unto them for ensamples: and they are written for our admonition, upon whom the ends of the world are come. (I Corinthians 10:11)*

While in the wilderness, Israel conducted themselves in an unfavorable fashion. Paul highlighted Israel's example in the wilderness in his first letter to the Corinthians. He described their activities which prevented the fathers from entering into Canaan.

Some believers, because of life's difficulties, are following the unfavorable example left by Israel. From Paul's discourse, we will examine Israel while they were in the wilderness. I Corinthians 10:6-10 records the example set by Israel.

THE GOD OF ANOTHER CHANCE

I. Israel lusted after evil things

II. Israel committed idolatry

III. Israel committed fornication

IV. Israel tempted God

V. Israel murmured/complained repeatedly

Through Moses, God said that He allowed Israel to wander in the wilderness to test them. It was to see whether they would obey God's commands. *The wilderness was not designed to keep them from Canaan but prepare them for it.* Because Israel failed to realize this, they committed the aforementioned indiscretions.

When a believer fails to understand that God wants to bless and fulfill His promise, he or she will follow Israel's example. Israel allowed the hardships of the wilderness to produce rebellion, murmuring, and sin in them.

Some believers today have allowed themselves to fall subject to sin through discontentment. Because of Israel's discontentment in the wilderness, they failed to believe God's promise.

Christians have to guard against this. Some who are reading this book feel as if their whole life is a wilderness. *They have received promises from God, but life seems to oppose the fulfillment of His promises. Because of this, they have lost zeal for Christ.* This leaves an open door for murmuring and rebellion, which will lead to sin as it did in Israel.

Israel paid dire consequences for their lack of faith. Instead of entering into Canaan, their children went in. Christians will experience this in some ways also.

THE GOD OF ANOTHER CHANCE

When we fail to walk in faith, we hinder the fulfillment of God's promise in our lives.

How? His power to do it is not hindered, but our sensitivity and faith in Him is hindered. *When this occurs, we will not obey Him when it is time to receive the promise.* This is what happened to Israel at Kadesh-Barnea.

But the men that went up with him said, We be not able to go up against the people; for they are stronger than we. (Numbers 13:31)

Moses led them to the edge of Canaan, but they did not have the faith to fight and possess. *When the believer doubts and complains, they will not have the faith to stand and receive what God has prepared for them.* Though the fathers did not enter into Canaan, God still fulfilled His promise to their children.

Israel's Entrance

Israel's ultimate entrance into Canaan serves as an example of encouragement to believers who have walked in doubt, frustration, and unbelief.

Though the fathers sinned and rebelled, God fulfilled His promise in the children. How does this apply to the believer?

> *And the Lord gave unto Israel all the land which he sware to give unto their fathers; and they possessed it, and dwelt therein. (Joshua 21:43)*

God will fulfill His promise even after we have complained, murmured, and sinned if we will repent. The children entered after the fathers died. If we allow complaints, frustration, depression, and sin to die within us, then we will be able to enter into our 'Canaan.'

God brought Israel out with the intent to bring them into Canaan. God delivers us from the bondage of sin to give us the life He has prepared for us. Because of this, He will be merciful to us while we are on our way to walking in His predestined plan for our lives.

From Israel's example, the believer has to remember to confess, repent and forsake sin, complaining, frustration, and bitterness. This is the only way the believer will go out of their personal "Egypt" and enter into "Canaan."

THE GOD OF ANOTHER CHANCE

Notes:

THE GOD OF ANOTHER CHANCE

THE GOD OF ANOTHER CHANCE

-Chapter 4-

Wilt thou be made whole?

THE GOD OF ANOTHER CHANCE

The man had been at the pool of Bethesda for thirty-eight years. Year after year, the angel of the Lord came down to trouble the water for the healing of the person who entered first. However, this man was in the right place, at the right time, but could not receive healing.

In this section, we want to examine this man's story. His story provides hope for individuals today who feel as if they have tried everything and still cannot get over past hurts, pains, and disappointments. In his letter to the

Philippians, Paul gives us a vital key to personal progress.

> *Brethren, I count not myself to have apprehended: but this one thing I do, forgetting those things which are behind, and reaching forth unto those things which are before, I press toward the mark for the prize of the high calling of God in Christ Jesus. (Phil 3:13-14)*

We must be willing to forget the things of the past. *Forget does not mean you do remember what happened, but that you let go of the negative emotions associated with what happened.* Yet, there is one more point to consider before we continue our discussion.

Within the context of Paul's statement, he understood that to gain Christ, he must forget his past success as a Pharisee and also his pure lineage as an Israelite.

Sometimes, past success can hinder us from present progress. Many live in the shadow of things they accomplished before and feel that they have let themselves and others down.

This is bondage. Hence, to enter into God's promises, individuals must let go of past successes to lay hold of what God will have for them presently and in the future.

From the man's story at the pool, we discover three truths to ensure personal deliverance from Egypt and entrance into Canaan.

Forget the Pain

The man was in need. No one had helped him in thirty-eight years, but Jesus appears offering a solution. He asks the man one question,

> *And a certain man was there, which had an infirmity thirty and eight years. When Jesus saw him lie, and knew that he had been now a long time in that case, he saith unto him, Wilt thou be made whole? (John 5:5-6)*

The man's response to Christ reveals he was still gripped by the pain of years gone by. Rather than answer in the affirmative, he recalls his troubles.

> *The impotent man answered him,*

Sir, I have no man, when the water is troubled, to put me into the pool: but while I am coming, another steppeth down before me. (John 5: 7)

Is this you? Do you constantly talk about why you are the way you are? Are you constantly discussing what happened? Do you always talk about how others are not there for you?

This was this man's problem. Jesus stood before him with help, but he could only talk about his situation.

THE GOD OF ANOTHER CHANCE

Many today are like this man. They have the same complaint: "You do not know what it's like for me; No one is there for me; No one understands me; no one listens to me!" Even if this is the case, Christ is not only there for you, but He is also listening. He has what you need.

Do not blame others for your lack of personal growth and freedom. Remember, when others fail you, Christ is a faithful Savior. Forgive those who have disappointed you and let you down. Let go of the pain of loneliness and being misunderstood.

Christ is asking you the same question now, "Will you be made whole?" Or, are you satisfied with complaining, depression, and personal isolation. It is unnecessary because Christ is there. Forget the pain of what has happened. In doing so, you can receive inner healing and peace.

Focus on Christ

When we let go of the pain of the negative events of our lives, we can receive from Christ. The man's story reveals that to forget the pain is not enough. We must then focus on Christ and His words.

> *Jesus saith unto him, Rise, take up thy bed, and walk. And immediately the man was made whole, and took up his bed, and walked: and on the same day was the sabbath. (John 5:8-9)*

It took only seven words from Christ (KJV translation) to deliver the man from thirty-eight years of physical ailment and emotional stress. When we focus on

Christ, our road to deliverance does not always need to be prolonged for He knows all things. He can do all things.

Oftentimes, the road to deliverance and inner recovery is more difficult than it has to because individuals lose sight of Christ and focus on what was rather than what is.

Remember, Peter walked on water as long as he focused on Jesus. If we want to escape personal bondages, our focus must be on Christ. Also, we must trust and obey what He says.

Christ gave the man instructions; when He obeyed, he recovered. When Christians trust the revelation of the Scriptures and the inspiration of the Holy Spirit, they will be able to escape any emotional and spiritual snares.

All scripture is given by inspiration of God, and is profitable for doctrine, for reproof, for correction, for instruction in righteousness: That the man of God may be perfect, thoroughly furnished unto all good works. (2 Tim 3:16-17)

THE GOD OF ANOTHER CHANCE

The Christian must trust that the scriptures are profitable for every area of their life. It equips them to do what is right. They will be able to escape from every place of bondage and live in victory.

Follow After Righteousness

One of the important aspects of this man's story must be addressed. After receiving his deliverance, Christ challenges the man in his personal life.

Afterward Jesus findeth him in the temple, and said unto him, Behold, thou art made whole: sin no more, lest a worse thing come unto thee. (John 5:14-15)

Remember, the focus of this book is to provide hope after failure. Jesus' words to the man reveal that the man's illness may have been the cause of some bad personal decisions.

If many are honest, certain present circumstances are the result of bad decisions and lack in one's personal walk with Christ. However, Christ provides a remedy. *It was not to condemn the man or to scare him. It was designed to keep the man in a place to maintain what he had received.* Christ wants us to remain free, even if we contributed to certain pains and troubles in our lives.

If we are to remain free from the failures of the past, we must continue to follow after righteousness. It is the righteousness of God revealed in Christ.

Even the righteousness of God which is by faith of Jesus Christ unto all and upon all them that believe: for there is no difference. (Romans 3:22)

It has nothing to do with religious

legalism, but it involves allowing the inner man to be transformed into Christ's image. This is how we follow after righteousness. If we allow ourselves to be transformed on the inside, our daily activities will reflect this.

We can be free. We can receive restoration after failure. God is the one who can bring clean out of the unclean things in our lives. He provided hope for Adam and Eve after they disobeyed. He provided protection for Cain after he murdered Abel. He remained faithful to

THE GOD OF ANOTHER CHANCE

Israel in the wilderness though they were rebellious. His mercy will prevail to those who continue on in Him.

Failure is not final. If our biblical counterparts could find restoration, then the Christian today can overcome. Success in the Christian life is possible. Forget the failures of the past and possess your destiny.

THE GOD OF ANOTHER CHANCE

Notes:

_____

_____

_____

_____

_____

_____

_____

_____

_____

_____

THE GOD OF ANOTHER CHANCE

Bibliography

Lockman Foundation. *Comparative Study Bible.* Zondervan Publishing House. Grand Rapids, MI, c1984

The Bible Library. *The Bible Library CD Rom Disc.* Ellis Enterprises Incorporated, (c) 1988 – 2000. 4205 McAuley Blvd., Suite 385, Oklahoma City, OK 73120. All Rights Reserved.

Merriam-Webster Online Dictionary.

Copyright © 2005 by Merriam-Webster, Incorporated. All rights reserved.

THE GOD OF ANOTHER CHANCE

Notes:

_____

_____

_____

_____

_____

_____

_____

_____

_____

THE GOD OF ANOTHER CHANCE

www.ingramcontent.com/pod-product-compliance
Lightning Source LLC
Chambersburg PA
CBHW050342010526
44119CB00049B/659